LIKE A GIRL: THE PRE-SHOW!

Layout & Design: Debbie J Cho
Editorial: Nancy Lynée Woo
Sarah Thursday
Terry Ann Wright

Lucid Moose Lit
Social justice meets the arts.

WELCOME TO *LIKE A GIRL: THE PRE-SHOW!*

We enthusiastically welcome you, dear reader, to a mini version—a teaser, a sneak peek, a coming attraction—of our book-length collection of poetry, prose, and art called *Like a Girl: Perspectives on Feminine Identity.*

We started by asking the question: What does it mean to say someone throws "like a girl" or cries "like a girl"? Why is being compared to a girl a derogatory mark? Is feminine identity subtly or overtly belittled in our society? We decided to challenge the assumption that being "like a girl" is weak or somehow "wrong," and instead honor the strength, beauty, and complexities of femininity. The theme was inspired by the Always commercial and their #LikeAGirl campaign (which, if you haven't seen, you should definitely look up on YouTube!).

Having received so many compelling submissions, we are proud to present some of them here (enamored as we are with all the great work we received, we just couldn't wait to show these artists off)! *The Pre-Show!* zine aims to stand on its own as a performance in and of itself, while simultaneously whetting your appetite for the main attraction. We look forward to you joining us for the anthology when it is released! You can find out more at LucidMooseLit.com.

Enthusiastically,
Lucid Moose Zine Team

TABLE OF CONTENTS
POETRY & PROSE

ART

~~~~~~~~~~~~~~~~~~~~~~~~~~~~~~~~~

INVENTORY

Elaine Mintzer

I want to write about nipples.
About nipples and doorbells,
but a girl at the next table is talking
about wetsuits and dry suits and underwear.
I want to write about things
sucked and thumbed
and travel on the other side
to France, maybe,
and Malaysia and Thailand and Africa.
I wish she'd shut up.

Nipples and doorbells.
And here is the problem:
even though the nipple
is attached to a breast,
and the breast is attached
to a torso,
to a woman
to a woman with a name,
somehow it is not the woman
who is kissed,
who is cupped in one hand,
whose belly is traced.
It is not her clavicle tongued,
her ribs counted,
the transmission is shot
and have you seen the turbocharged
discrete components,
and whether we call it nipple or breast,
we don't call it me.
Me with a name
on the couch with the remote
ignoring everything:

I name myself.

I am. All the body parts.
Flat tire, dented fender,
piston and spark plug.
'92 Astrovan.
Toes, knees, vulva.
Me.

Angelica Nuñez

WHAT I MEAN WHEN I SAY NIECE Danielle Mitchell

Elaborate zoology. Wheat-grower's nose, my mother's spitfire pistol, sister's technical austerity, my hair. Genetic rope. One frayed end for each blonde strand. I mean, falling apart while filling in. The best kind of imitation. Ears, chin and the perfect bow of a mouth learning to drink from a straw. Chain reaction. I mean, the equator of me split open and pouring out tropical storms, one for each eye color. Glorious repetition. A chorus. A gaggle. A bouquet. Something bred through the mind; crack in the skull most acutely. I mean, harvest of girl. Perfect cornucopia. Seven times blessed. Each watchtower in the city aglow. Landscape with tricycle and plume. Glitter army. I mean, hope for the world. I mean, pigtail, milkmaid, waterfall, rope.

3

for Allison, Lauren, Brittney, Nicole, Ashley, Kirsten, and Aubrey

JELLY GIRLS

Sarah Thursday

In 1984, every girl
wore those jelly shoes.
Glitter plastic in pink
          and blue and yellow,
seemed so frivolous.

          They hurt, they pinched,
gave no heel or arch support,
but still,
          I wanted them.

Flimsy buckles and basket-
          weave spilling toes out,
          leaving sharp red grooves
like a map for hours.

4

I wanted to be that frivolous,
          to let them squeeze the surface of
my nine-year-old feet, marking me
like every girl.

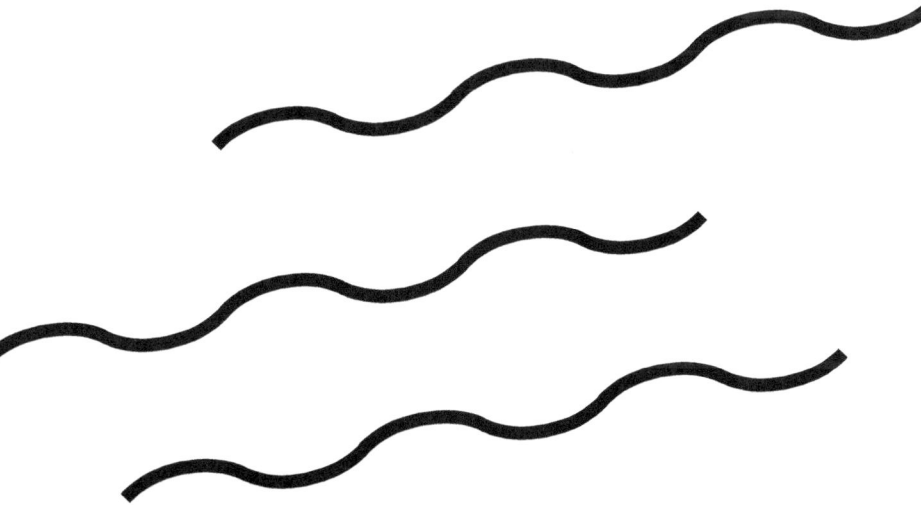

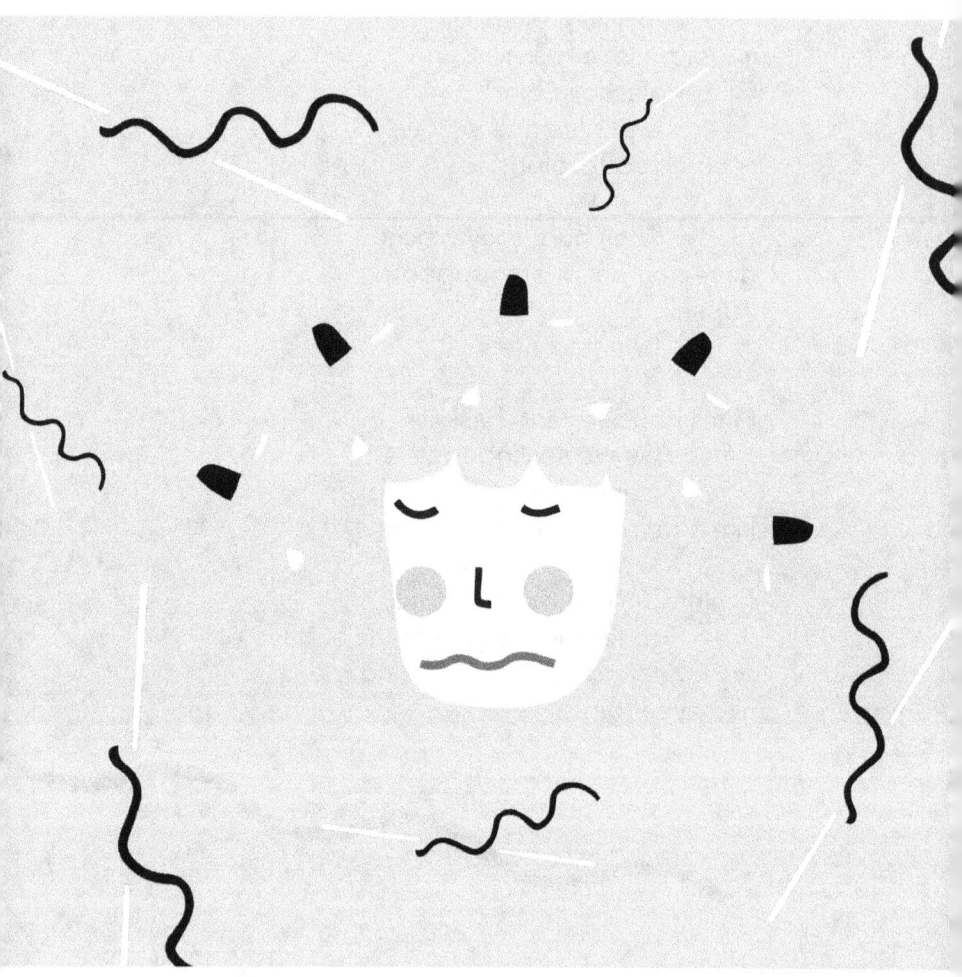

Debbie J Cho

LITTLE MISS METAPHOR

Don Kingfisher Campbell

Studying out the window
in my pickup truck
soon-to-be-four
Kyla queries

"Daddy,
trees need to be cut
like people's hair, right?"

We pass the San Gabriel Mission
on the way to Grandma's house
and Kyla proclaims

"There's Notre Dame;
Quasimodo's house."

In my mother's living room
Kyla observes the Jesus
figurine in a glass case

"It's Daddy!"

My sister's self-portrait
hangs over the sofa
"That's Pocahontas."

Kyla looks up   6
to the neglected ceiling
and images water spots

"Mira, Mami,
patas de cucui. "*
That night
on the drive home

"Mami,
I love you in the sun,
I love you in the moon."

*(in English, "Look, Mommy,
monster feet. ")

Alexis Rhone Fancher

TEGAN, SARA

Keayva Mitchell

When we were eight,
or maybe nine,
you and I wrestled in the space between
the cherry foot of your bed,
and the dirty, fraying edge of your purple throw rug.
My magic spot of Anything Goes,
where you accidentally aligned your girl parts
with my girl parts,
so I touched my tongue to your clavicle
just to see how you tasted –
and you scratched my face so that I bled
and never looked at me again.

I told her about you, once.
She let me nibble, peck, graze over pink nipples –
over smooth curves – over dark places.
She is not you,
but the hard ridge of her collarbone tastes as reckless.

Our alignment is never accidental.

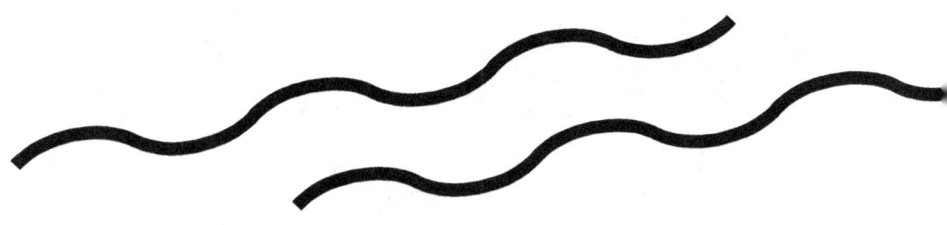

JACARANDA SONG

Kelsey Bryan-Zwick

Debbie J Cho

down the street at Jackie's, in her yard
we play dolls, purple in the tea cups
sipping petals inside her playhouse, sweet stick
on the tongue, I keep eyeing the dogs
Jackie's dogs, they are huge, and pacing outside
the plastic window, bodies bigger than the frame

they are all jaws and sharp teeth
the terror of raptor clash claws
their muscled breathing fills my belly
the dogs, they are looking at me
pushing the little red door open
someone has filled my ankles
with stones, running against
the weight of myself
and the dogs, they chase me
they'll rip me like a possum
carry me bloody like a rat

Jackie's yard ends, I can't stop running
scrape against the pavement
and those dogs, larger than before
are on top of me
I need them to bite me
scratch me from my sparkle-tank
my place is quiet, mommy's
at the hospital, alabaster

the room where everyone is small
getting radiated behind a lead
wall, so sick, even the nurses
can't touch her, I cannot feel my body
the baby is skinny, on formula
my brother sings in his sleep
mommy has a bump in her boobie
bump in her boobie, I do not hear
dad's been crying at the bar

and the dogs won't bite
won't chew up my bones
only lick my skinned knees
sitting there on the patio
waiting for a band-aid
all I can see is their sharp teeth
they are daggers, spiked
bloody with my blood

PUBERTY

Natalie Morales

How else can the world know you're a woman

-unless-

that first black strand pops up in your armpit
along with its pubic cousins building
fortresses like it's medieval times

-unless-

bra shopping
having to learn the
social repercussions of
the Letter A

-unless-

shaving with dull pink razors
from the 99 cent store
drips of blood in the bath dilute
(Is that why girls like pink so much?)

-unless-

that odd look in mother's eye
a cross between suspicion and relief
when you tell her you figured babies were made that way.

But hey,
the reward comes
when you get to use PMS
as an excuse
for yelling with your mouth full
and cramps as an excuse
for just about everything.

AT TWELVE,

Alexis Rhone Fancher

O! backyard see-saw,
days spent courting
steel between my legs,
the thrilling rub
that knew no name.

Forgive my mother,
turning from the window;

Forgive my father,
highball in hand;

Forgive my uncle,
hiding in the juniper hedge
hand down his pants;

Forgive me my
furious pumping,

oblivious,

the curious damp
an addiction,

a glimpse of my future.

CRAVING

Donna Hilbert

I broke the long stems
of dry spaghetti
into worm-sized pieces
that I ate as I watched
cartoons on TV:
Baby Huey in his tiny diaper,
Porky and Petunia Pig.
I popped the round top
from the Hershey's chocolate can,
spooned the unsweetened
powder into my mouth.

Danielle Zamora

Mom was pregnant.
At my eleventh birthday party,
Dad patted her belly,
bragged to my friends
that he'd *blown up that balloon.*
It was the beginning of summer.
My friends had begun to kiss boys,
steal candy and cigarettes
from Vons.
I spent the long afternoons
lying on the floor,
cartoons flickering silently
on the black and white TV,
the cord of the telephone
wrapped around my arm,
whispers of the high school boy
I knew from the park
slipping into my ear.
I ate the skin
from the tips of my fingers,
from the tops of my toes
until they bled.
I didn't know then
what was bitter,
as my life spilled out around me,
fine powder from a dark brown tin.

NO THANKS TO GOD Karla Cordero

Before the sun laid its hands across cornfields
before men & straw hats picked cabbage

my mother's womb rivered me into this world
screaming thunder.

I was born with a back made of bricks,
a mouth full of tumbleweed & desert cactus.

Skin so tan
it wrapped around my bones like sweet caramel.

Mother prayed for me she did.
15 Plucked rosary beads for fourteen hours.

Too afraid of this world
where little girls with broken English

forget how to speak
their way back to their mother's dinner table.

Where colors
brown & blood sound too familiar at funeral.

This world waiting
for baptism to break the flames.

Mother still prays to every moon, every ocean
to swallow my body.

Asking Noah's flood to shatter my lungs
hoping chaos

never knocks at my door
begging for a glass of water.

VAGINA DENTADA ARMADA

JL Martindale

My father refers to us as The Cunts
militant but brainless, a species
of legs and shark-toothed vaginas
that glisten, though jawless,
beasts bent on devouring his soul.

16

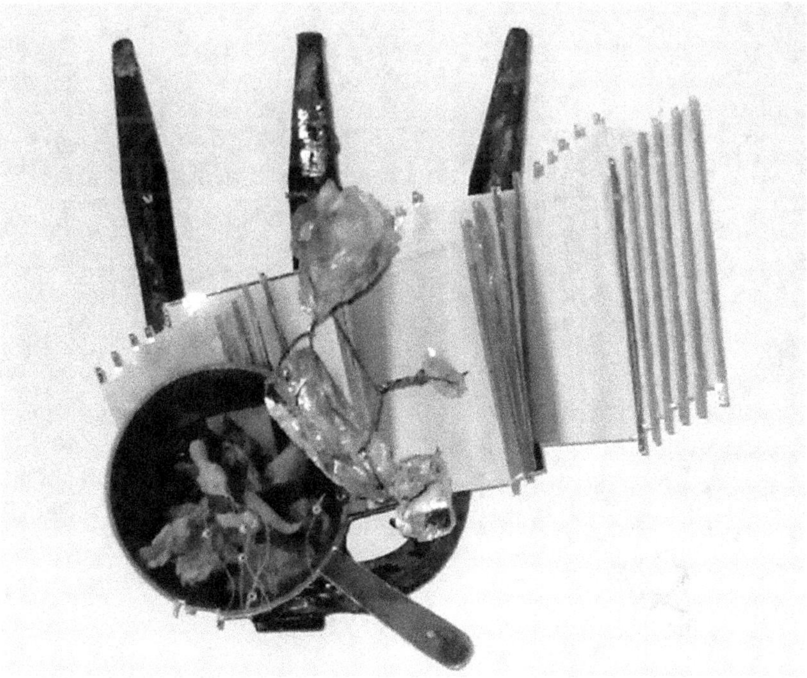

Toti O'Brien

TALKING HEAD Lee Kottner

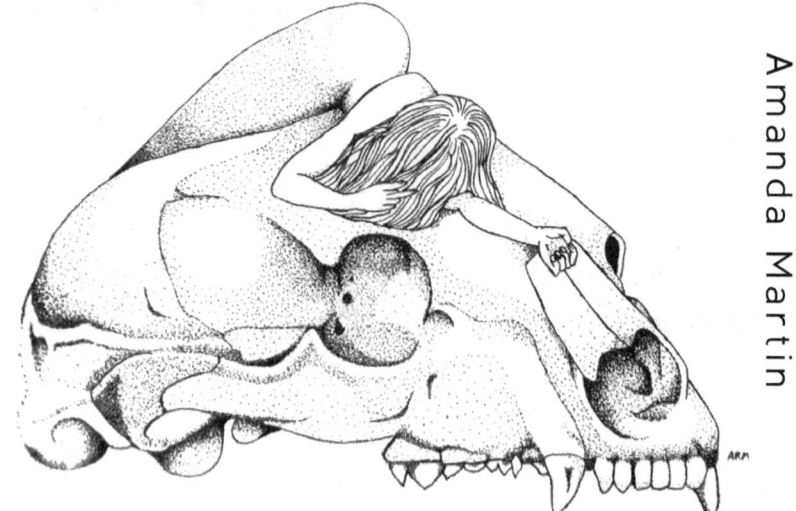

Amanda Martin

It's too hot to bother.
I walk through fountains and hydrants gladly, I would
take off my shirt—like you with the hairy
belly overflowing your belt—grumble
at wearing one more piece of clothing
underneath. But it might be too provoking
not to.
Uptown, downtown, we stand on the subway platforms.
Sweating.
All of us. And she, unmindful
of the old shackles of lace
and wire, whalebone
and silk,
wears as little as she can

high above the knee,
just below the round curve of
her hips and ass.
She has a fine body and pride in it.
This is her favorite dress,
not chrysalis or shed skin, just
the choice she's made today.
New-skin tight,
it moves with her
long strides, loose-limbed
and tight lipped,
umber cotton over café au lait.
Below a lengthy column of thigh and calf:
cowboy boots tooled with the care of tattoos.
Her hair is unleashed in wild
curls of humidity.

I can hear her father, her boyfriend, the
proprietary men in her life:
Dress like that, you're asking for it, girl.

How is she asking for . . . it?
In the elevator,
does she reach down your pants
grab that thing
and say *gotta have it baby*?
Does she walk up to you in the street
pleading, *please say something intimate and crude*
about my body
to the world at large?

Oh. It was the dress. I see.

Then it wasn't you said those things either.

Must have been your cock
talking.

CHRONIC HICCUPS

Elmast Kozloyan

Help help help help
Help help help help help

It didn't even sound like a word anymore
Everyone thought I had developed chronic hiccups
They told me I should
hold my breath
drink water very quickly
and stand upside down
      All at once if I could
Nothing helped
helped help help help help help

When the sun set
or the lights dimmed

Fernando Gallegos

Help help help
When a man's gaze lingered help
too long help help help help
When a coat sleeve help
brushed my help help
skin help help help help help

Air escapes me
like I want to escape me
like I want to escape
like I did
the day I couldn't
I couldn't help myself

No one could

I GET A TATTOO Ricki Mandeville

A frog, I tell the tattoo artist.
My sister gapes, looking stunned—
she expected me
to choose something pretty,
something with wings:
a Painted Lady butterfly on the pale leaf
of my shoulder
a long-forelocked Pegasus
springing skyward from my upper arm,
at the very least a ladybug
poised cutely above my ankle bone,
gentle creatures gifted with flight,
little works of art to grace
the pristine canvas of my body.

But I say *frog*, not once considering
the bulging eyes, the lumpy skin,
never taking into account
the unattractive connotations:
the incessant croaking,
the possible warts,
the sticky tongue's grim ability
to yank an unsuspecting bug from its
tiny insect life and make of it a meal.

My friends will wonder *why on earth*
but I'll say nothing, won't divulge
my bedtime-story notion
that where there's a frog
there might yet be a prince.

21

MACKINAC

Terry Ann Wright

ISLAND

for Cheryl

In the photograph we are
stacked neatly on some wooden steps:
mother in her tidy blue pantsuit,
sleeveless even then, long before
anorexia starved every last curve from her bicep.
We ate fudge, which was a special treat,
but what do I remember of eating it?

Sitting on some steps, peeling thin wax paper
from blocks of fudge, puzzled by such good fortune.
Puzzled by being allowed to do something
we weren't ever supposed to do.
I think we waited to be punished for eating it,
not for it to be slapped out of our hands,
but for disgust to be conveyed by pressed lips
and a simple turn of the head.

Touch her now and she's strings and wire.
(Why starve your breasts away at 77?)
Am I just too much flesh to take at once?
She begs for hugs, but even then
stands stiffly, pulls away sharply.
Maybe she just wants to see how my shoulder blades feel
under her gnarled hand. The pet, pet, of a witch
robbed of all powers because she can't bear to eat.

22

MAMÁ MAKES HOMES Marco A. Vasquez

Dressed in a white smock spotted
with blue-petaled daisies, she
vacuums the living room—bright
with the curtain filtered afternoon
rays. Rag in hand, she dusts the mantle

and television, lifting candle
holders, family photographs, and—
onto a gentle palm—crucified
statuettes. Funny how dust can
accumulate in an unused

room—dad always working, children
married into new families
or education. It must fall
from the popcorn ceiling, as we
sleep, clinging to nurturing memories.

She scrubs porcelain toilets, tubs,
and sinks with detergents
and sanitizers as unfamiliar
to dad and me as feminine
hygiene products. She's tended

unmade beds—blankets left in mounds
on the floor—and picked-up yesterday's
clothes left piled at the closet's base.
With slippered feet, she begins
preparing a meal, three hours

in advance, using the arsenal
of small appliances that she's
received during the holidays—keeping
track of cook-time for the sake
of simultaneous completion

to ensure fresh dishes and large
portions—slapping together *masa*
into fresh tortillas, and grinding
roasted *chiles* and tomatoes
into a rich pulp, even though

both products are easily available
in prepackaged containers. It's too
late to settle for simplicity.
She goes from room to room, with
the meticulous detail of a drill-

sergeant—keeping an orderly home,
that goes unnoticed by dad and me—
already accustomed to the accommodations—
as we come home after rush-hour,
unlock the door, and storm into

the kitchen where she has set—
on a place-mat, beside a napkin,
knife, fork—a plate steaming with colorful
piles of sustenance, that disappear
in seconds, hardly tasted, barely

chewed—flavors rediscovered during
the after-math of explosive
nasal-burps—thanking her with grunts,
sighs, and belly-rubs, as we sit
back and watch her do the dishes.

WOMB

Amanda Martin

There is a history never
learned because women have
been treated like a mystery,
emotions too complex for man

to understand—language of
Venus is hysterical. Hysteria
was the diagnosis given to
the misses who were forced

into rest until they changed
the paper on the walls to
sparkling citrine stalactite
and stalagmite, to crawl inside—

amniotic bath healing, no
false labors, born again
they tore down the walls
of the crimson tissue with you.

SURGERY

Nancy Lynée Woo

Grab the scalpel.

Today is the day
I cut out my uterus.

The computer processor
upstairs will know how.
We will be so much better off
without the whining and complaints
and the *thud thud thud* of the
laundry room of the body.

I've been thinking about it for
centuries, ever since I learned
how to read the contours of
*his*tory and found no place
for her. All she does is cause
problems for the motherboard.

We don't need yogurt and berries or
off days and menstrual cramps or
mood swings revolving around
chocolate. Not in this work force
that feeds us beef and gin.

I've got some things to say
without crying.

I want to make it here.

In developing the web of my mind
I've found this code to be a nuisance.
The software glitches.

Hand me the knife.

It will be better this way.
Time to turn down the soft hum
whispering, *Listen*. Press your ear
to the earth to feel its pulse.
Listen. For children and magic.
Scoop your hands in the dirt
and pray for rain.

Yes, it will be better this way.

It's time.

I'll finally pillage without remorse, enjoy
stealing the treasures of others, and stop
worrying about what is being destroyed
that can never be replaced.

I'll join all the boys' clubs and
smoke myself huge and expand
outward until everything I touch
is my kingdom. I will forget
to lay in wait for the dull to pass.
Howl without regret and stop listening
for the return call.

I will no longer busy myself about things
to cherish. Be free from the nuances
of overwhelming love. Life may soon
not feel so urgent.

Please, pass me the blade.

I never claimed to be brave.
I am only tired and it is time.

I need a way to resolve the brain and clit,
mind and breasts, paradox
of flesh. My hands are able
to hold a hammer. My feet

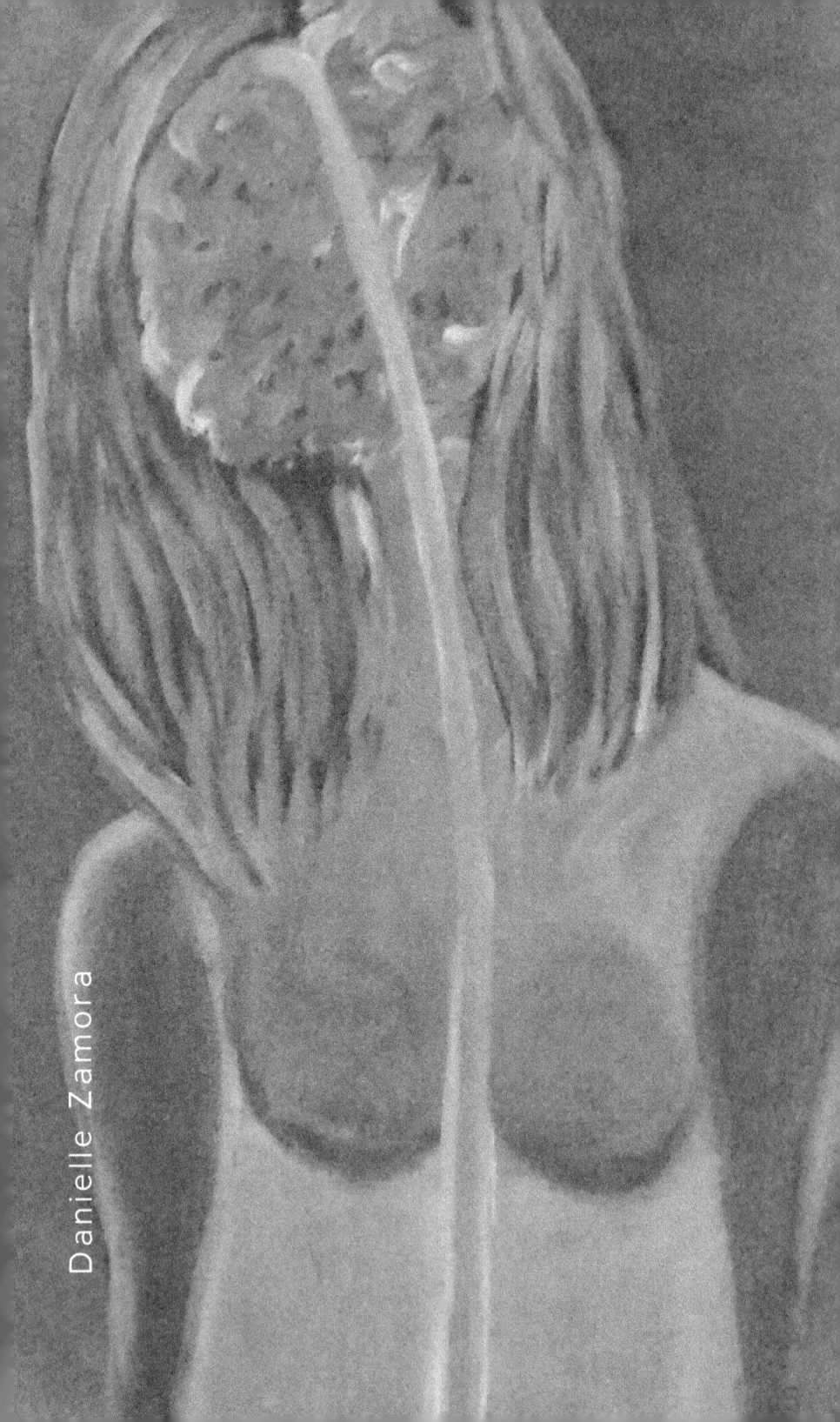

Danielle Zamora

still delicate and small. My mind
sharp as a cut.

Pray for my daughter it is cleaner
than this.

That she'll be free from fear
not a rabbit caught in a trap
a runner with no gun
a whore on the streets
with a fire in her eyes.

I pray for my daughter,
and I don't even pray.

My daughter. The blade.

Mind sharp as a cut.

This may

have to wait.

Listen: I can hear her out there somewhere.

Here, just give me the knife.
I'll hold onto it, keep the sharp
edge safe by my bed so when my daughter
feels the pulse to end the trick
of her life, she will know
to come to me first.

And I will tell her:
You have more to give.
You have more to give.
You have so much more to give.

WONDER WOMAN,
UNDERWEAR?

Raundi Moore-Kondo

Fernando Gallegos

I got them for 2 bucks
on the discount rack at Fashion-For-Less
and wear them when
I want truth and justice for all
or get the urge to tie someone up

When I need to deflect bullets, chauvinists
and women who hate women
who look like women they don't like

I wear them when I want to perform my own stunts
When flying invisible planes, defeating Nazis
or holding a bass line down is a remote possibility

For chasing ninjas across rooftops
For walking red carpets and sleeping in tents
For fighting crime, grime and time
For making your world a more wonderful place

I can run ten times farther
than The 6 Million Dollar Man
at one trillionth the price

I can style my hair higher
and disarm the armed
without decapitating anyone

With them I am more Wonder
and more Woman
More cotton-spandex, stretch
and super-hero support
Cross my heart
Stars and Stripes forever
I may never take them off

OUGHT

Emilie Staat

Elderly ladies ought not to wear onesies. Particularly, they ought not to wear cheetah-print onesies. At least, Olive didn't think so. She thought that ladies of a certain age ought to have more dignity, more graciousness of person. Unfortunately, Mellora *did* think a cheetah-print onesie (with décolletage, no less) perfectly appropriate attire for women such as themselves and she'd spent the week crafting the costumes for the Laurel Hills Retirement Community's Halloween Mixer. Rather than hosting the event in the community room of the main building, where they sometimes had yoga and ceramics (and once, an embarrassing bellydance lesson taught by a pert twenty-year-old with more core muscle control than a normal person ought to have), LHRC rented the ballroom of the local Hilton just for the occasion. Oh *how* had Olive allowed Mellora to talk her into this pathetic excuse for clothing—did anyone really want to see the flesh that was revealed and the curves that were hugged, at their ages? It would've been bad enough in the privacy of the community room, amongst their saggy, moldering peers. But here it was, broad daylight, and children were trick-or-treating (as they ought to be doing) in their own costumes as Mellora and Olive (who had no right to be out dressed like this!) drove past them in Mellora's decadent and gaudy pink Bug (really!) wearing cat ears and whiskers. And yes, there were tails. Tails! No one could see those just yet, but their tails would be seen, sure enough, before this hellacious evening was finished.

"Oh buck up, Olive. These costumes are jaunty," Mellora declared, her whiskers twitching above her lipsticked mouth. Redder lipstick than she ought to be wearing at her age.

"Halloween just isn't what it used to be," Olive murmured, helplessly watching in utter mortification as all the little jaws dropped open in enormous astonishment.

Daniel McGinn

THE BODY LANGUAGE OF LOVE AND HATE

Angela Moore

35

Girl: what can my body do for me?
Dance. Climb trees. Outrun my brothers.
I don't really notice it unless I burn my hand on the stove or
skin my shin on the brick porch steps. I like when mom softly
scratches my back until I fall asleep, or wakes me up with
kisses. I love my body!

Adolescent: what the hell is happening to my body?
It's getting lumpy. I got blood on my too-tight pants.
Mom bought me a bra to hide my nipples. Why are people
looking at me? Why are they touching me? Why do they
comment on my changing body? I starve then binge.
I hate my body.

Young Woman: what can my body do for you?
I will shave it. Pluck it. Even suction my insides out.
I will wear this. And I will do that. Even if it hurts. But I'm
tired of starving, so I won't do that anymore. And those
pills are making me sick, so I won't take them anymore.
I can start to take care of my body.

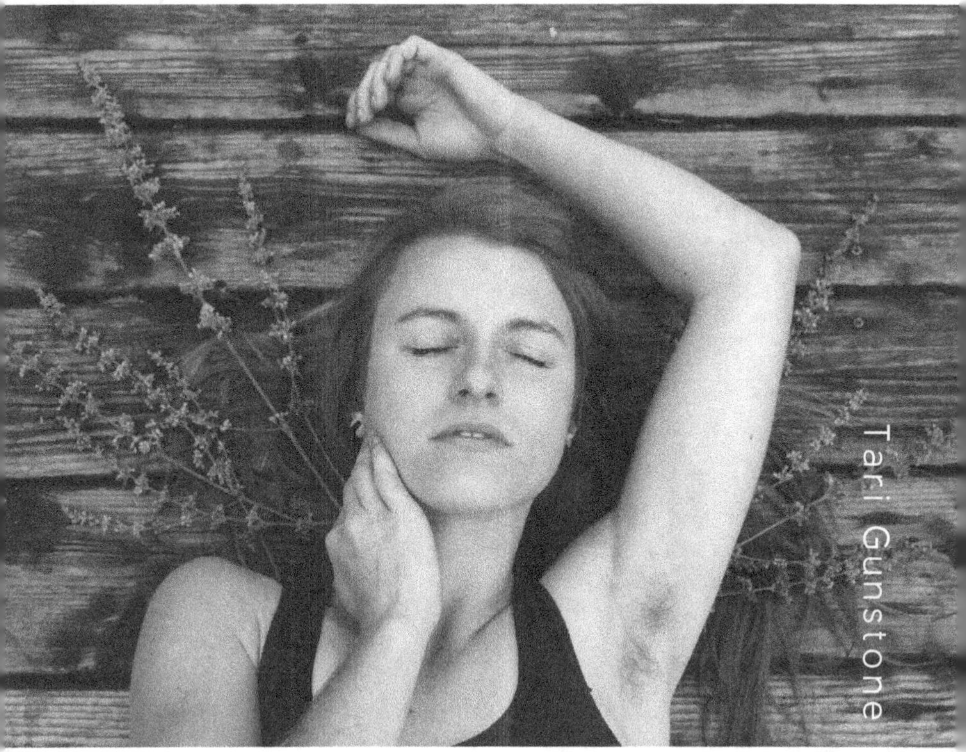

Taril Gunstone

Mother: what the hell is happening to my body?
Nested in blood, cells combine and then divide.
My body and the new one know what to do and
enable growth. My systems support developing systems.
How ever did I dare criticize such an amazing body?

Woman: what can I do for my body?
Listen and meet its needs. Nourishment,
movement and rest. Hugs and kisses. Sunshine and
bare feet. My gaze caresses every new line and growing
asymmetry, my hand every scar and dimple.
I love my body.

CALIFORNIA

My soul is a chaparral, surviving despite the drought.
These hills flourish, reborn after each annual brush fire.
Purified, strengthened by native smoke of white sage.

Those scrawny coyotes shivering in your headlights
are my reckless, desperate sex.

Witness these cunning birds of prey:
my condor, my falcon, my Golden Eagle
salivating over your imminent demise
your greed caught in my ruthless talons.
You used me.

I bathed you with poppy sage hills,
with the awe of my wingspan.
My native oaks shaded us
from the life-sucking sun.
You basked in my watercolor sunsets
atop mountains with ocean views
that shimmer far brighter
than your city of artificial light.

SAGE

JL Martindale

But that wasn't good enough.
You demanded complete surrender
while you raped my riverbeds for gold
before bringing your backhoes and bulldozers
shaving, reshaping my land.
You erect concrete and steel towers
antennas and asphalt on my virgin hills.

You carve my earth and call it yours.
You strip me of my nature
then curse me when my flames rise
charring your paper deeds,
your claims
    dissolve
     to
    ash
swept and scattered
by those indifferent Santa Ana winds.

I will not surrender
(anymore).
This chaparral will once again thrive
when San Andreas opens her thighs
    and swallows
       you whole.

Debbie J Cho

I HEARD WHAT SOUNDED LIKE A SONG

Ellyn Maybe

It sounded like la.
I started to hum with the knowing melody.
Suddenly the voice got louder
and it didn't sound like la anymore.
The voice said live.

I looked around and there was Joan of Arc.
She said Leonard Cohen got me right.
Music is the highest calling.
She said live.

I know it's not easy being a woman who knows
the difference between Gene Kelly and Gene Krupa.
Miles Davis and Miles Traveled.
I know how men make women wear armor of all kinds.

It's natural to think of blowing out your candles.
When you read Tennessee Williams,
many things go through one's mind.

It's hard to watch angels go to bed
with wings and in the morning it's ash.

Dreyer got it right.
The soul is in the eyes.
Close-up.

She said I'm a trick candle.
They think they extinguished me,
but I never completely go out.
Live.

My body is not my soul. Of course not.
I know martyrs from all times and seasons.
We play mahjong in Heaven, we read comic books.
We are not 24/7 serious.
That's what really scared them.

Every them through history is afraid
of what's brimming and can't be controlled.
When she spoke, smoke came from her mouth
like the grate of a Manhattan street.
Like a dragon.

She nodded it's my DNA now.
My descendants wherever they may be.
They will recognize each other.

Of course we can tell the chain smokers from the saints.
We are not naive.
Everyone wants a puff of immortality without having to die.
Death is a passing fancy.

40

Still for one glittering moment,
I wanted a knight in shining armor to rescue me.
Like Guinevere and Lancelot.
But I was King Arthur.

My hands were tied.
I assure you, I miss the grass
I used to walk on barefoot.
My feet were so much dust so quickly.

I was a girl who played hopscotch.
I was a girl who picked berries and had little girl crushes.
I was a little girl.

Live hung in the air like the notes you hear
after the opera is over.
The reverberations last forever.

AUTHORS & ARTISTS

Alexis Rhone Fancher's collection of erotic poems, *How I Lost My Virginity To Michael Cohen and Other Heart Stab Poems* (Sybaritic Press, 2014), is available on Amazon. "At Twelve, The Awakening" first appeared in *How I Lost My Virginity To Michael Cohen & Other Heart Stab Poems*, Sybaritic Press, 2014.

Amanda Martin is a feminist artist from the Inland Empire. She is perpetually in the process of unravelling her cocoon.

Angela Moore is currently in a rock band, staging a new musical, singing to hospice patients, and loving her musical men.

Angelica Nuñez has been a writer and an award-winning artist for over 20 years, residing in Long Beach, CA.

4| **Daniel McGinn**'s poetry has been seen in numerous publications. This is the first time he has had a found photograph published.

Danielle Mitchell directs The Poetry Lab in Long Beach, CA. Her work is forthcoming in Harpur Palate, H_NGM_N, and Bellevue Literary Review.

Danielle Zamora is a Mexican-American woman, a self-reflective painter, singer, and lyricist with a double Bachelor's in Art and Psychology.

Don Kingfisher Campbell hosts the Saturday Afternoon Poetry reading series in Pasadena. For publication credits, please go to: http://dkc1031.blogspot.com

Donna Hilbert's work is widely anthologized, most recently in The Widows' Handbook, Kent State University Press. Learn more at www.donnahilbert.com. "Craving" first appeared in *Transforming Matter*, PEARL Editions, 2000.

Elaine Mintzer grew up in the Valley, attended college over the hill, writes in a coffee house near the beach. "Inventory" first appeared in *Natural Selections*, Bombshelter Press, 2005.

Ellyn Maybe, United States Artist nominee 2012, performs solo, with her band and her duo project, ellyn & robbie. ellynmaybe.com. "I Heard What Sounded Like a Song" first appeared in *Praha and the Poet*.

Elmast Kozloyan is a writer trapped in limbo between magic and reality (though seldom chooses the latter).

Emilie Staat is writing a memoir about learning how to dance tango, and a novel. She lives in New Orleans.

SoCal artist, **Fernando Gallegos**, is inspired by the human form and attempts to evoke the feeling of movement and emotion.

JL Martindale writes stuff. Her poetry has been published with Cadence Collective, Bank Heavy Press, Lucid Moose Lit and more.

Karla Cordero is a Loft Literary Fellow and Editor of Spit Journal. Her first chapbook, *Grasshoppers Before Gods*, releases in 2015 (Dancing Girl Press).

Keayva Mitchell is a 22-year-old poet living in California. She enjoys buttons, pastries, being awkward, and you.

42

Kelsey Bryan-Zwick is a poet from Long Beach, CA. Her second chapbook is due out in 2015 (Sadie Girl Press). "Jacaranda Song" first appeared in *Poems by Sunday*.

Lee Kottner is a writer, educator, union activist, and book artist living in Harlem, NY.

Marco A. Vasquez was born and raised in East Los Angeles. His first novel, *Steven Isn't Normal*, was recently published by Floricanto Press.

Natalie Morales is a master's student at Cal Poly Pomona and creative writer of poems focusing on love, lust, and loss.

Raundi Moore-Kondo has become everything she ever wanted to be: poet, teacher, singer/songwriter, business owner, publisher, wife, mother, and bass player in a punk band. www.TheLoveOfWords.com. "Wonder Woman, Underwear?" first appeared in *Attack of the Poems*.

Ricki Mandeville lives near the beach, where it never snows, except in her poems, which have appeared in various print and electronic journals.

Photographer **Tari Gunstone** and Herbalist **Bailey Kelly-Burger** started Woman in the Raw, a project creating conversation about natural femininity. womanintheraw.tumblr.com

Toti O'Brien is an artist, writer and performer, also known as the Italian Accordionist, with an Irish last name.

LIKE A GIRL: THE PRE-SHOW! TEAM

Debbie J Cho is a photographer and visual artist currently based in Los Angeles. www.debbiejcho.com

43   **Nancy Lynée Woo** is a 2015 PEN Center USA Emerging Voices Fellow and co-founder of Lucid Moose Lit. NancyLyneeWoo.com.

Sarah Thursday is co-host of 2nd Mondays Poetry Party, editor of CadenceCollective.net, founder of Sadie Girl Press, and co-founder of Lucid Moose Lit!

Terry Ann Wright has two Pushcart Prize nominations but is kind of more famous for her legendary hosting of Pajamarama! StoryTime.